To my Nana Eileen who at thirteen years of age had her own school days cut short by the Second World War when she was evacuated from London. She is one of the most intelligent people I know despite her lack of school years and I love her dearly.

MOVING UP

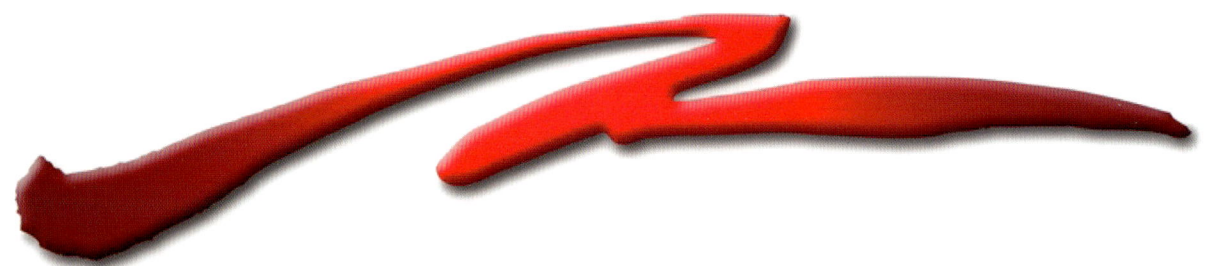

We all know it's hard, moving up from primary to secondary school, but it's something everyone goes through. It can be tough when you're suddenly way out of your comfort zone and forced to start from scratch, making a new group of friends and mastering more complex secondary skills.

There's always going to be a bully lurking somewhere, a teacher that picks on you or a little group that ignores your pleas for acceptance, but with this book and a little self belief moving on to secondary school should be easy.

Leaving books - Many primaries let you buy a book as a leaving gift and it's really useful to purchase something which will be of use at secondary school. So put back that riveting read from the fiction pile and get over to the reference shelf. If you have a computer then a dictionary or thesaurus might be a waste, why not try for something subject specific like a science dictionary or ICT key words.

WARNING

. . . you might find you're drowning in your school uniform as your Mum decides to get her money's worth by buying clothes for you "to grow into"

Uniform - When you're buying a new school uniform don't leave it too late. If you go at the start of the summer holidays and buy the full kit, then nearer to September, try all your uniform on again. Then if you have grown the shop can just swap over the things that you need to change for a different size. Also, it is pure madness in the shops the closer you get to the start of term so allow plenty of time for the trip.

FOLLOW THAT BUS

It might be the first time that you will be taking the bus to school as most people tend to live nearer to their primary schools. You could either make the journey in the holidays just to test it out and note where your stops are en route or at least check it all out virtually on the Internet. Check with your friends to see who else might be taking the bus and also check with the school to find out if you have to get a bus pass or pay for individual journeys.

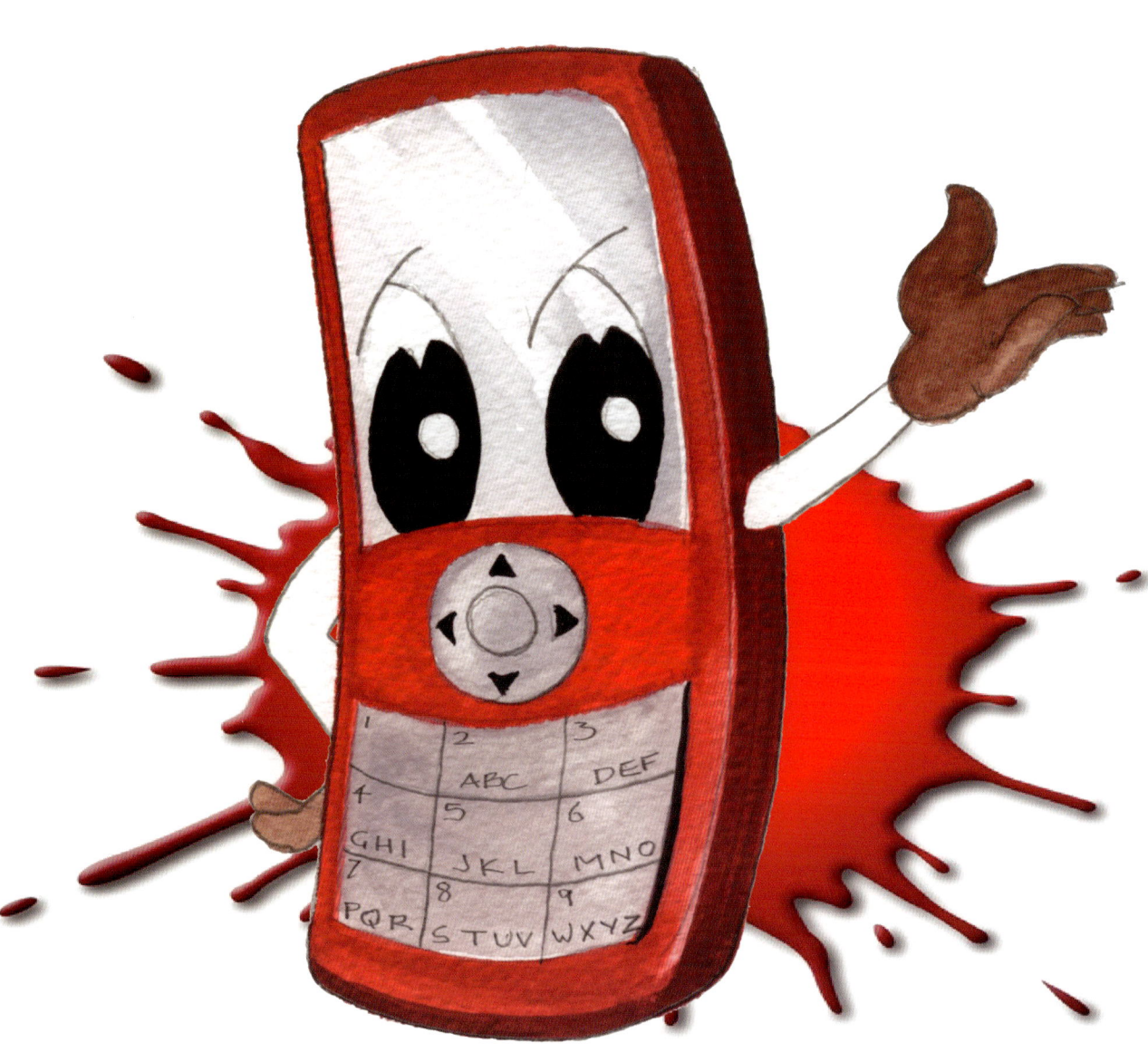

Mobile phone - If you decide to buy a mobile phone for when you go up to year seven it's always a good idea to key in your emergency contacts before the start of term. That way if you miss your bus or have to stay on after school you will be able to contact your parents, guardian or friends to let them know what's going on.

COUCH POTATO

Although it may be great to have broken up from the day to day routine of your old school and all you want to do is veg. out in front of the television it would be a great time to squeeze in some studying too. I know it sounds really boring but whenever you go shopping look out for some books about some of the subjects you will be studying at your new school. Even if you were the cleverest student at your old school you may find yourself thrown in at the deep end with peers who are of a higher ability than you in some of the subjects that you thought you were the best in. If you wish to maintain your straight 'A' streak you may want to delve into the odd reference book or start surfing the net for some light research on your future subjects.

OUTRAGEOUSLY ORGANISED

Be well prepared, pack the night before not in the morning when you're more likely to be in a rush and forget something. Trust me; you don't want to forget to pack your school books or your PE kit on the first day! Anyway it can be really exciting to unwrap all you're new things in readiness for your first term.

Research - It is human nature to resist change and be frightened by things we are unfamiliar with so it's a great idea to swot up on your new school. Read the booklet they provide for new starters and visit the school website to see what you can find out, there will be lots of information about opportunities for students. Before you know it you will feel more a part of the community of your school.

The sorting hat experience - Waiting to find out what house you're in is very Harry Potterish. Once you know, swap email addresses and MSN contacts with the people you meet on your induction day then you can get to know each other online and perhaps arrange to meet up before you start in the September. It's kind of scary turning up at a new school without knowing anyone so it's a great idea to at least have someone to talk to which will help you settle in.

UNDER PRESSURE

At this time more than any other I think we feel under pressure to fit in and of course this is a big deal, but try to be yourself and you will make some genuine friends, possibly for life.

Join a club - Although you are bound to make some special friends it's always a good idea to have a back up plan as if you fall out with one of your friends you will always have someone else's shoulder to cry on. A great way of making new friends is to join a club and try and chat to some of the people you are working with which should be easy as you both probably have lots to say about the activity you are doing.

OUT WITH THE OLD IN WITH THE NEW!!!

You may have friends from your primary moving up with you to the secondary school but it doesn't mean that you have to dump them when you get into year seven. It will help to have some familiar faces in your form room but at the same time don't restrict yourself just to those classmates you already know. Secondary school is on a much bigger scale so there will be lots of people who might become even better friends than those you had at primary.

Mule bag - For the first few months you tend to carry ALL of your books around with you because you are terrified you might turn up to a lesson with a fearsome teacher and realise you have forgotten their subject books. A good way to make sure this never happens is to invest in a decent bag to carry everything about; otherwise you'll be looking like Quasimodo by the time half term arrives. Also you could pack all your books in a locker and only put the books for the next lessons until break or lunch in your bag.

BAN THE BULLY

Any incidents, verbal or physical, report them straight away. Not only are you protecting yourself and others, you are highlighting the problem that the bully may be facing and you could be helping to stop them from repeating the behaviour. Those people who engage in bullying are often the victims of bullying themselves.

LOVE YOUR LOGBOOK

Spend some time getting to know the layout and the useful extra pages you didn't realise existed. During the term, note down your homework and any reminders to yourself about bringing in kit or money for trips. Use highlighters or coloured pen to help the information you record stand out.

Be yourself always - At this time more than any other I think we feel under pressure to fit in and of course this is a big deal, but try to be yourself and you will make some genuine friends. If you try to act differently just to be accepted in a group then you'll be constantly stressed and strained, which is not a healthy state to be in. If you make true friends they won't ask you to go against your own judgement.

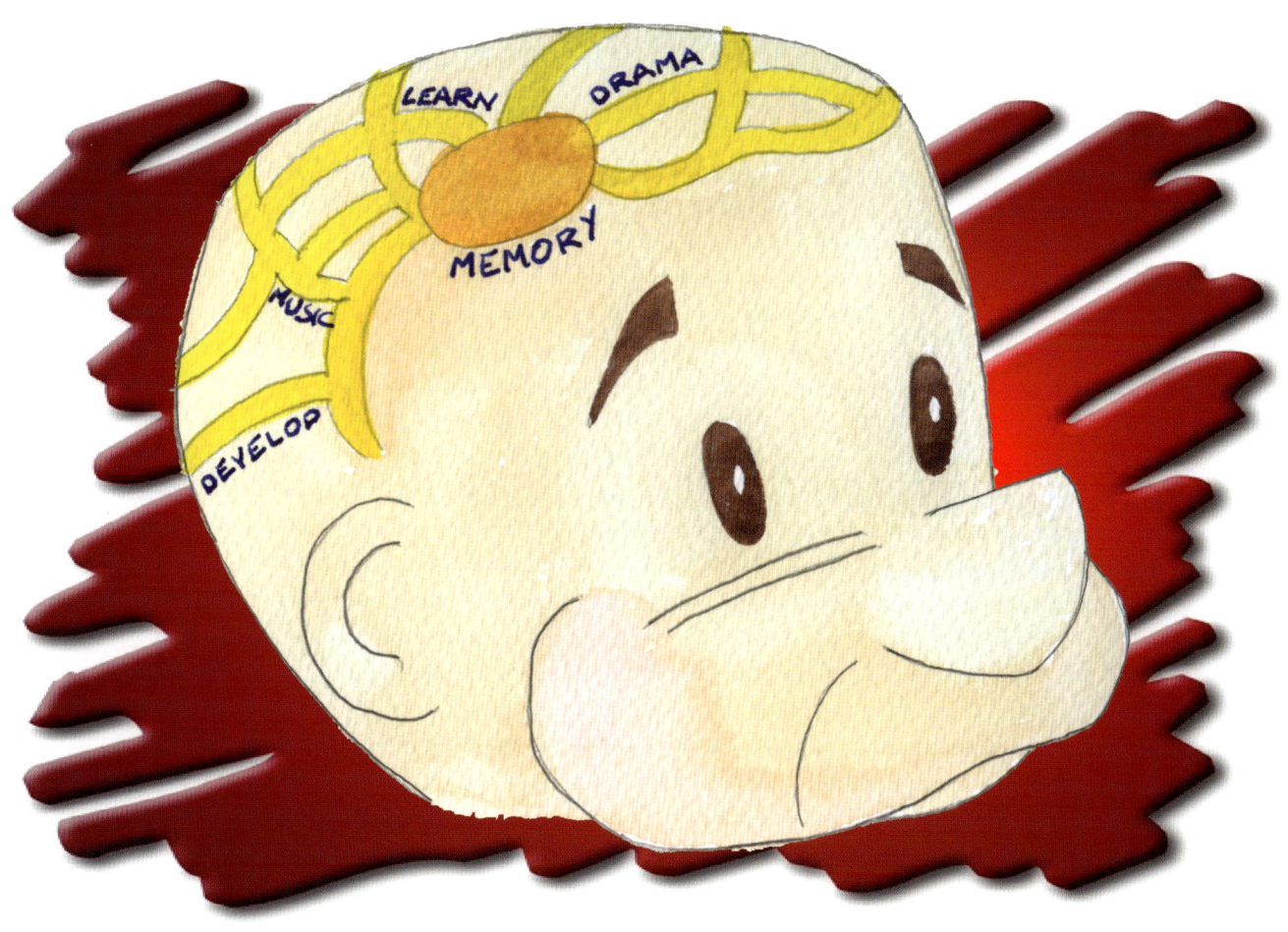

Do a mind map for the year ahead – If you set down on paper now what you hope to get out of your first year at secondary school then you will have a much better chance of achieving your goals. You'll be amazed when you look back after your first year at what you have achieved.

BE PREPARED

A spare small purse or wallet with your emergency stash can save you a lot of hassle. I mean what are the chances that you'd lose both of them on the same day? Keep it in a separate section of your backpack, just in case.

School dinners??? v Packed Lunch???
It can be hard to decide whether to have cooked dinners or a packed lunch but really it doesn't matter too much as long as your getting enough to eat and what you are eating will keep you awake all through last period. Remember fatty foods will give you short bursts of energy, but carbohydrates and fruit and vegetables will last you throughout the day which is ideal for school! If you still can't decide which meal choice to have try to vary it during the week and keep hydrated by drinking lots of water.

TALK IT OVER

September 1st lunch with a friend, a good way of talking through any last minute concerns and checking you've covered all the bases. Also, helps to mark this major milestone with a treat.

Try a musical instrument - It's always great to discover a new talent and maybe you can if you take music lessons at your new school. You'll find that at secondary level you will have a lot more specialist teachers so it will be a great opportunity to enjoy either one on one, or group tuition learning an instrument you've always dreamed of playing!

HOMEWORK HASSLE

Do your homework on the night it is set. This way you don't have it nagging away at the back of your mind. If you do it straight away then it is over with and will be ready whenever your teacher asks for it to be handed in. Sometimes one late homework can stay in the back of a teacher's mind even if you get them all in on time after that, but don't worry too much if it happens just the once it's always hard on your first week to adjust to the amount of homework you get and there is sure to be a sympathetic teacher somewhere in your new school.

THERE'S ALWAYS ONE

There's always one teacher you just can't get along with. Okay so we are all different and their teaching style might not suit your learning style but life is like that and it's best to try and focus on the subject rather than letting a personality clash put you off altogether.

Watch – If you haven't got one then now is a good time (no pun intended) when you're out on the playing field or trying to work out how long you've got to the end of the lesson, you'll wish you had one.

Support your classmates – If you go out of your way to assist other people in your class rather than just focusing on the fact that everything may be going well for you, not only will you be recognised as a friendly face but if ever in the future you need a helping hand it is more likely that the people you have previously supported will want to comfort you.

FRETTING FOLK

It's only natural for your parents to worry about you and maybe as far as you're concerned too much. But think about it - as hard as it is to believe they've gone through all the same experiences as you, they are just concerned that you don't have to face any problems you might have alone. Give them a break and for your sake as well, when you are relaxed and comfortable spare a few minutes to tell them about your day. If you want to go the whole hog then maybe ask about their's as well!

Ask questions - Don't be afraid to ask questions. Believe me teachers will be relieved and so will most of your class mates if you ask the question that is on everybody else's lips. What is the point of sitting in class wasting time because you would feel more stupid to put up your hand and ask one little question.

ESCAPOLOGY ACT

It's a great idea to concentrate on your school work and revise whenever you have the time but you need to keep a balance. One way of doing this is to find a hobby that isn't too challenging and won't drain lots of your energy. This way you can escape and completely focus on what you are doing.

Two weeks notice - well not quite that much but give parents plenty of notice when you need particular items for school, such as ingredients for food technology, materials for design – it will cause you and them a lot of grief if you suddenly realise the night before you are lacking the resources required for lessons the next day.

EXCELLENTLY EQUIPPED

Try out any new pieces of equipment that you have acquired, such as your scientific calculator and moulding your gum shield ready for PE. Don't forget those routine things like sharpening coloured pencils for Art and stocking up on ink cartridges for your fountain pen in English.

Sorry skivers – Whatever you do no matter how tough you may find school at first don't skive. An education is really important and will help you get a better job when you're older, plus it can be hard work catching up on the lessons you miss. Remember that there are millions of children in countries torn apart by conflict that go without an education every day. They don't have a choice but you do.

TRY TRIPPING

There are bound to be trips for a variety of different subjects in year seven and some may even be residential. Sign up for as many as you can because not only will you have the chance to learn outside the classroom walls but it will be an important part of bonding with new friends.